I LOVE MY COLOR I'M IN

By: Daisy Copelin

Colors, Colors everywhere so many beautiful skin colors that I stop to stare.

So many skin colors it's so perplexing but what gives us our skin's complexion?
2

Melanin is the reason to be, you see,
but what is Melanin? Melanin is the pigment
that gives our hair, eyes and skin its color.

3

The more melanin you have the darker your skin color the less melanin you have the lighter your skin color.

Take a look at your skin color. Do you have more or less melanin?
5

Whether I have less melanin or more my skin color I love to adore it.

ABC

I love my skin color. It's dark, the opposite of light and closely resembles the color of midnight.

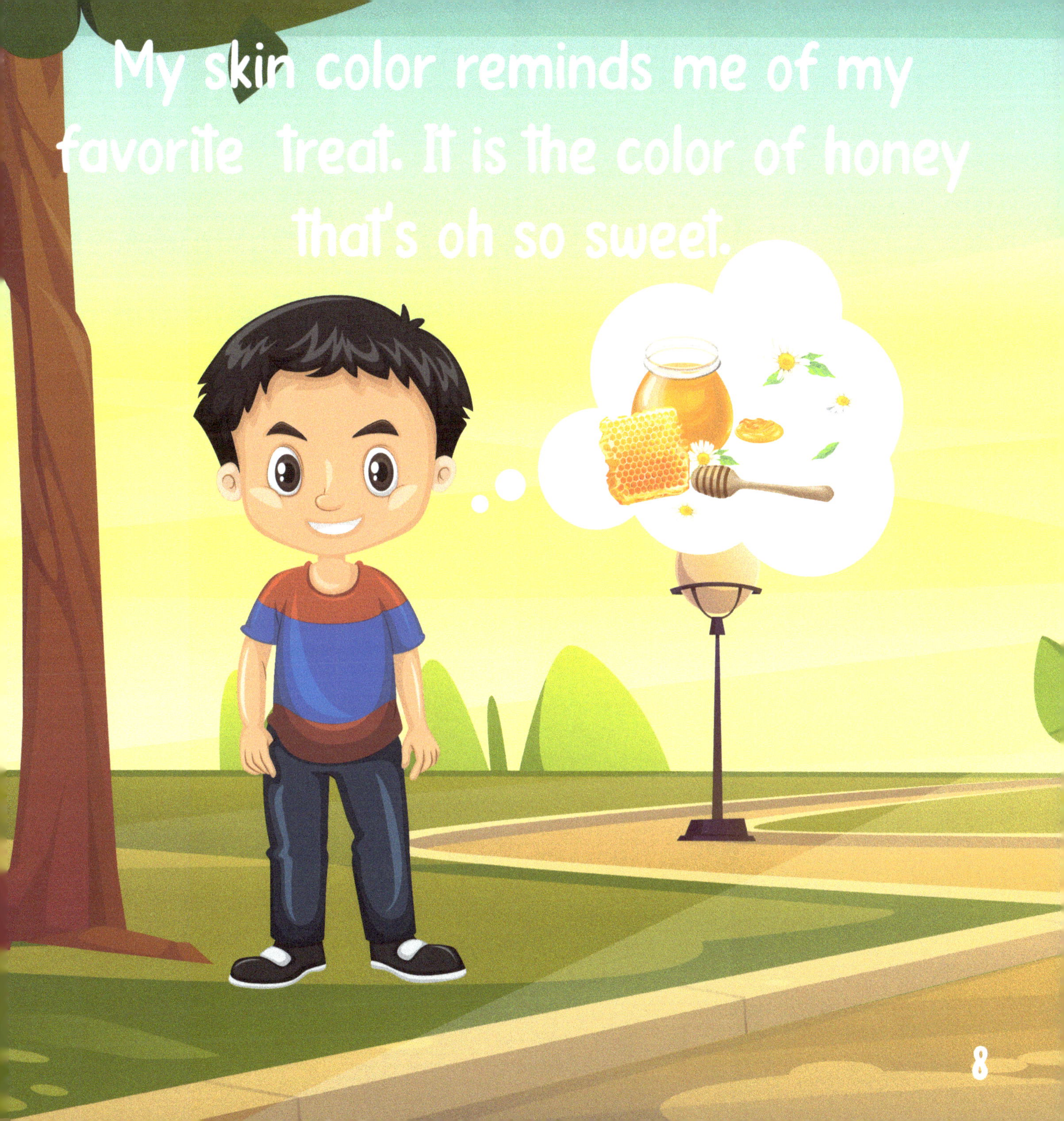
My skin color reminds me of my favorite treat. It is the color of honey that's oh so sweet.

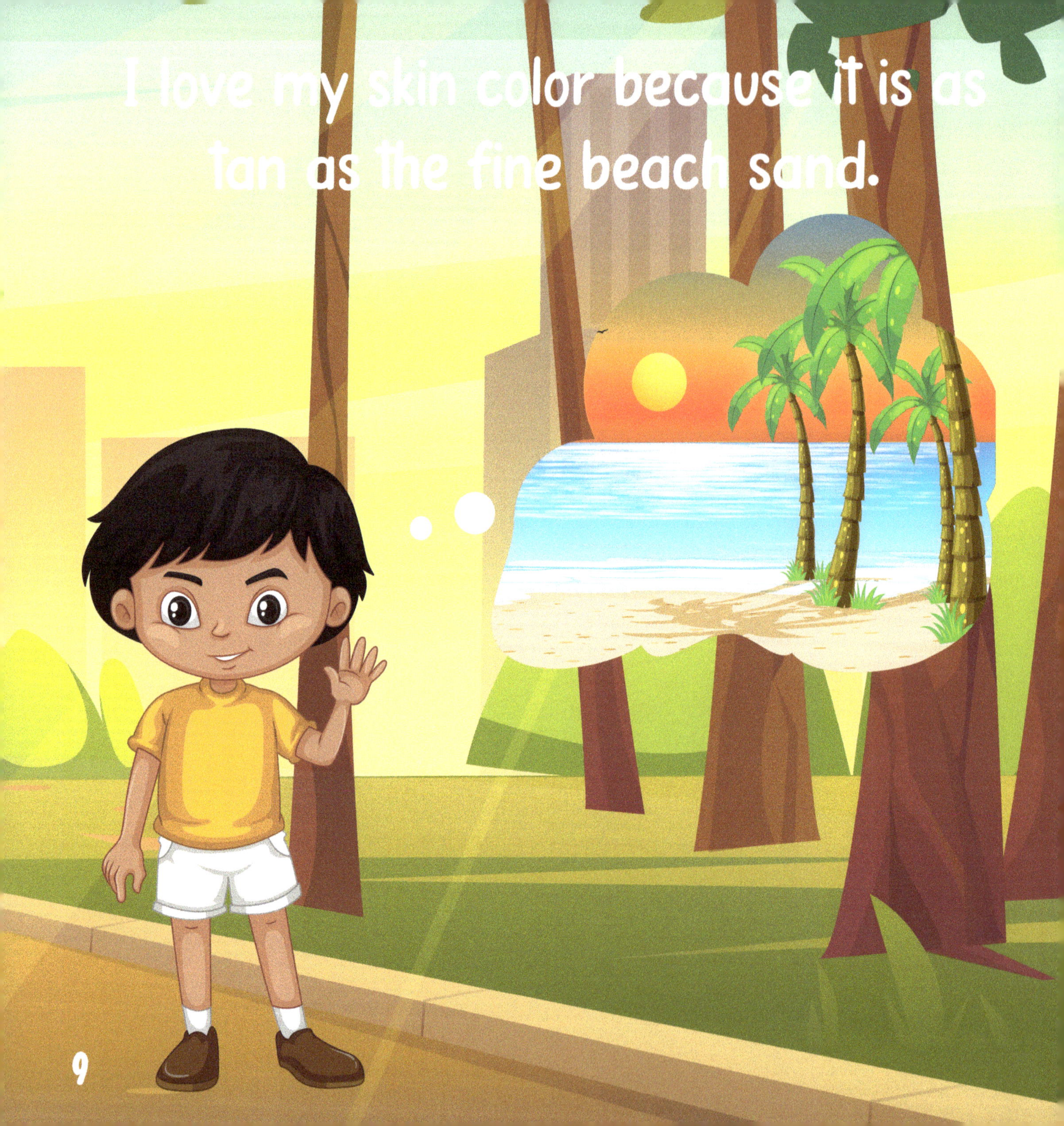

I love my skin color because it is as tan as the fine beach sand.
9

Whenever I see my skin color I like to boast because it reminds me of the color of my lightly brown colored morning's toast.

PEANUT BUTTER

10

I love my skin color because it's fair and closely resembles the color of the inside of a pear.

11

I love my skin color because it's brown.
I also enjoy looking in the mirror at
myself and my skin color as I pretend
to be a king in a crown.

I have albinism but I love my skin color, which means less pigment which makes my skin color very light close to white.
13

I love my skin color because it reminds
me of a peach that is oh so yummy
when it goes into my very hungry
tummy.

I love my skin color because it's a beautiful mixture of brown. When I look in the mirror I pretend to be a princess as I twirl all around.

Colors, Colors everywhere so many beautiful
skin colors that I continue to stop and stare.

Whenever I want to run around and play with my friends I go to the park. Some of my friends' skin colors are light and some are dark.

17

What matters the most is not the color of your skin on the outside but by how kind you are inside

No matter the color of your skin your aim should be to always treat everyone how you wish to be treated the same.